Trojan Barbie

by Christine Evans

A SAMUEL FRENCH ACTING EDITION

SAMUEL
FRENCH
FOUNDED 1830
NEW YORK HOLLYWOOD LONDON TORONTO

SAMUELFRENCH.COM

ISBN 978-0-573-69867-5   Printed in U.S.A.   #29658

MUSIC USE NOTE

IMPORTANT BILLING AND CREDIT
REQUIREMENTS

TROJAN BARBIE was produced by the American Repertory Theater in Cambridge, Massachusetts, on March 28, 2009. The performance was directed by Carmel O'Reilly, with sets and costumes by David Reynoso, lighting by Justin Townsend, sound by David Remedios and dramaturgy by Gideon Lester and Katie Mallinson. The production stage manager was Chris De Camillis. The cast was as follows:

HECUBA . . . . .Paula Langton

POLLY X . . . . Kaaron Briscoe

CASSANDRA . . . . .Nina Kassa

ANDROMACHE. . . . . Skye Noel

CLEA . . . . .Emily Alpren

ESME . . . . .Lisette Silva

HELEN. . . . . .Careena Melia

LOTTE. . . . . Karen MacDonald

MICA . . . . Renzo Ampuero

TALTHYBIUS/MAX. . . . . Carl Foreman

JORGE/MENELAUS/CLIVE/OFFICER IN BLUE . . . . Jim Senti

CHARACTERS

The Trojans

HECUBA – Queen of Trojans; widow of Priam.

POLLY X – Hecuba's youngest daughter, age 15.

CASSANDRA – Hecuba's prescient daughter; late teens.

ANDROMACHE – Hecuba's daughter-in-law; Hector's widow; early 30s.

CLEA – Woman in the camp; CHORUS. Age can be flexibly cast.

ESME – Woman in the camp; CHORUS. Age can be flexibly cast.

The Others

HELEN – The face that launched, etc. Ageless.

LOTTE – An English tourist and doll repair expert. Age 35-50.

MICA – Camp guard; also assigned to local spin. 30s.

JORGE – Soldier from the conquering army. 20s. Latino.

MAX – Soldier from the conquering army. 20s. African-American.

MENELAUS – Helen's slighted husband; led the army that destroyed Troy. 30s or 40s.

CLIVE – Lotte's fantasy partner (actually a waiter.) Ageless and perfect.

OFFICER IN BLUE – Deus Ex Machina from the conquering army.

TALTHYBIUS – Diplomatic African gentleman; messenger from the conquering army. Age can be flexibly cast.

Note on double casting

The roles of **MENELAUS**, **CLIVE** and **OFFICER IN BLUE** may be played by the same actor. At the director's discretion, the same actor may also join the action as a **SOLDIER** (without lines) in Scenes Eleven and Fourteen.

If necessary, **MAX** and **TALTHYBIUS** may also be double-cast, but if resources permit, it's preferable to cast these as stand-alone roles.

SETTING

Mythic Troy; modern Troy; and Lotte's doll hospital in England.

TIME

The past, folded uneasily into the present.

AUTHOR'S NOTES

The Trojan women's camp is a barren space that suggests both ancient and modern war zones. The sparse presence of elements such as cyclone wire, plastic sheeting, or rusted corrugated iron sheets evokes contemporary refugee camps.

There are other spaces: a space of the gods where Polly X and Cassandra at times appear; Lotte's doll hospital in England and the tourist café she visits in contemporary Troy.

There is a sense of an archaeological dig, as if time were stacked vertically in layers of ruin, with modernity at the top layer on the surface. Since layers of time collapse into one another in this play, it's best served by a flexible and evocative design, where discrete spaces can form and bleed into one another, rather than being "realistically" rendered.

Note on punctuation: A slash (/) indicates the interruption point in a line by the following speaker.

ACKNOWLEDGEMENTS

Sincere thanks to all those who supported *Trojan Barbie* in its development:

Roberto Gutiérrez Varea, Peter Novak, the Performing Arts and Social Justice Program at the University of San Francisco, ¡El Teatro Jornalero!, Ann Woodhead, Marisela Treviño Orta and Santiago Perez; Paula Vogel and David Konstan; Rick Massimo; Charlotte Meehan; Vanessa Gilbert; Pat and Ernie Evans; Synchronicity Theatre and the SheWRITES Festival; Catherine Coray, Daniella Topol and the hotINK International Festival of New Plays; Megan Sandberg-Zakian, Nadia Mahdi and the Providence Black Repertory Company; Rob Melrose, Jayne Wenger and Cutting Ball Theater's "Risk Is This" Festival; Resonance Ensemble; Joseph Megel and the Process Series at U.N.C. Chapel Hill; Gail Evans and Ciella Williams; David Kaye and the University of New Hampshire's cast and crew;Peregrine Whittlesey; Robert Scanlan; Gideon Lester, Carmel O'Reilly and the 2009 cast and creative team at the A.R.T.; and the many gifted actors who generously gave their time in readings and workshops.

This play is for my niece Ciella Lee Williams

*and for all the girls who'd rather invent something
than be icons:*

A love poem from the past to your future.

Scene One

(Lights up on **LOTTE***. We are in* **LOTTE**'s *doll hospital workshop. Beside her are shelves of doll parts and broken dolls in various stages of repair – some are contemporary; others are older porcelain models. One shelf has a series of these older dolls sitting in a row, looking a little like the bodies from war photographs. Some stare out from empty eye sockets. Others are missing limbs, heads, hair.* **LOTTE** *is tidying up, getting ready for her trip away.)*

LOTTE. Horse-hair. Acrylic hair. Sandpaper. Latex. Legs. Ball sockets. Eyelash glue…Damnit, I've run out of eyes again. Better re-order before I leave. *(to an eyeless doll)* Sorry.

(checking travel wallet) Now, what *mustn't* I forget…

Passport. Imodium. Aspirin. Cellphone charger!!! Emergency numbers –

(turns to glossy brochure) "Claude's Cultural Tours for Singles – A Great Way to Meet People!" – People are nicer on holiday.

(shuffling through her brochure) "Romance in Rome"… no… "Catalan Cuisine"…same old, same old…Here we are! – "Tragedy in Troy!" *(reads from brochure)* "Troy is rich in history. The city has been razed and rebuilt nine times, each time resurrecting itself over the buried bones of its previous lives and deaths." Mmm, that sounds cheerful… – Oh, cut it out, Lotte. You need to get more involved in life. I'm sure it will be lovely. *(to the dolls, firmly)* It will be lovely.

(Cross-fade from **LOTTE** *space to* **POLLY X***, who is in a separate, elevated space.* **POLLY** *and* **LOTTE** *are in different worlds.* **POLLY** *wears a school uniform.)*

POLLY X. Everything stinks here. I hate it. It stinks because we have to use *gas* for cleaning. Even the hospitals. For cleaning floors, toilets, wounds, everything. You can't get soap any more. And since the fence, you can't even go out. There's nothing to do. It's foul. This whole country is like a poisoned stinky gas station just waiting for someone to throw a match. I am sooo over it.

Oh, I want to smell desert rain again. It hasn't rained for three years. It's probably because we're cursed.

Anyway. Before the fence, Mama took me to the museum so I would see our "Cultural Heritage." But it was all looted, except for the Contemporary Art. So – we had to look at *that* instead. The program said that "Transcendent Ideas of Beauty" are no longer what art is about. But actually, I just think we can't afford it. Like I said, it's hard to get stuff. So most of it was really ugly, and all made of broken things. Or things that really aren't supposed to be art. Like bottles and rags and old shoes and stuff just stuck together.

The most disgusting sculpture of all was called TROJAN RAT. It had yellow eyes, and it was crouching in a pool of dark stuff that looked like oil, or blood or something yukky. And it was hollow; you could see inside it because it was just made out of wire and plastic bags. Inside its belly it had a little white dining table, all tiny and perfect like real art. There was a family sitting round it, eating dinner.

But their house was bleeding and it was inside a rat.

Which had mean glittery eyes made of those yellow beer bottle tops that the soldiers leave lying around.

It made me feel sick but excited, too.
I didn't like it but I did. I didn't but I did.

Mama hated it. She said it was "decadent and defeatist."
I said, Well Hecuba, we are defeated.

She didn't say anything to that.

And then I decided: I *like* Modern Sculpture.

POLLY X. *(cont.)* On the way home, I started thinking about things I could make out of my own broken stuff. Mostly what I've got is these –

(showing Barbie dolls)

Most of them are a bit messed up, or they're covered in scribble and stuff.

Which is OK for Modern Sculpture.

I'm going to get a big piece of pink cardboard. Helen says if you're nice to the soldiers, they'll get you stuff. And then I'm going to get all my dolls and nail them onto it. In the shape of a big heart. So when it's finished, it will be this huge heart, made of smashed up dolls. It will be sort of flat but sort of three-dimensional. It will be very, very scary. I'm going to hang it out the front of the women's tents.

And I'm calling it TROJAN BARBIE. And when it's done, me and Cassandra will rain down revenge on our enemies! We will smash them like dolls! Death to the invaders!

*(Loud rock-music clip. We are in **POLLY**'s Xena / Buffy the vampire slayer / Britney Spears fantasy. A huge pink heart materializes behind her. **POLLY X** stands and holds up a haphazard fistful of Barbies / Barbie parts, dances with them. Lights dim til she is a back-lit silhouette against the brilliant pink heart.)*

(Then from offstage, through distorted megaphone, we hear:)

JORGE. Polly X. Polly X?

*(Crossed spotlights, like stereo hunting lights, focus in blindingly on **POLLY X**.)*

POLLY X. What? Who's that?

JORGE. Princess Polly Xena. We have orders to escort you to Achilles' tomb for the purposes of ritual sacrifice. Do not resist. Place your hands above your head. Drop your weapons.

(POLLY X drops the dolls.)

JORGE. Are you still a virgin?

POLLY X. What? – Fuck off!

(MAX and JORGE approach POLLY X.)

POLLY X. Mama! Mama, help! Help –

> *(Hunting spotlights switch off. POLLY is a silhouette again. JORGE and MAX drag her off, covering her mouth to stifle her screams.)*

Scene Two

(HECUBA wakes with a start as POLLY screams. We are in the camp. There are tent walls or sheets hung upstage, making a scrim. They are back-lit and the bodies of women are visible in silhouette through them.)

HECUBA. POLLY! Polly X – ? – Clea? What was that? Clea? Esme?

ESME. Nothing.

CLEA. A riot, maybe. Or thunder.

ESME. An old pot smashing.

CLEA & ESME. Something breaking.

HECUBA. A heart cracking its own ribs with fear.
Something blind –

HECUBA, CLEA & ESME. – beating against the bars of a cage.

(Lights up, dimly, on LOTTE's space. LOTTE is absorbed with her dolls, checking things. HECUBA senses her presence. The others don't.)

HECUBA. My children are mixing with the dead
Burning in the oil of their own future
Lighting the Underworld.
Their breath on my neck's so close, I turn, then wake –
To this
To this –
A world that can't be dreamed without them.

CLEA. Hecuba, you're dreaming on your feet again. You need to sleep.

HECUBA. Sleep's too close to death, Clea. We need to stay awake for the living.
Even when it seems hopeless.

LOTTE. *(consulting her list)* Oh, this is hopeless –

HECUBA. But Gods/ where was I?

LOTTE. Where was I?

HECUBA. Back in the hospital again. Or the morgue?

LOTTE. I can't read my own handwriting.

HECUBA. I can't tell any more.

LOTTE. "S." Sun block. Hand sanitizer. Swimsuit. Sunglasses. Spare SIM card. *(pause)* Mosquito-net? – Oh come on Lotte, it's not the Congo. Troy is in Europe – sort of.

ESME. Perhaps it won't be so different, where we're going. If we live, that is.

CLEA. Perhaps we'll be sent somewhere warm. Comfort women have to live in comfort, don't they?

ESME. Yeah, but slaves don't. Probably end up in a sweatshop with fourteen-hour shifts.

CLEA. And in your "time off" you can service the boss and do his wife's ironing.

*(**CLEA** and **ESME** exit.)*

HECUBA. I'm sorting through the bodies again
they're heaped in the corridor.
I'm always here when I dream.

LOTTE. *(to dolls, taking inventory)* And as for you lot…

HECUBA. But this time there aren't even bodies, just limbs
hopelessly mixed up –
An old man's ear, a girl's left hand –

LOTTE & HECUBA. – Hair, heads, legs, fingers –

HECUBA. – I can't find her.

LOTTE. – I can't find anything. *Eyes.* I must reorder eyes.

*(On her next lines, a quiet litany, **LOTTE** fades from view.)*

LOTTE. Toothpaste. Tylenol. Tampons. Tickets!! Travelers' checks. Tic-tacs.

HECUBA. My children dead or vanished
My boys murdered, my girls –
Where are my girls? Polly?
– Cassandra!

(**CASSANDRA** *dances out of the tent like a firecracker. She sings the first two lines of the chorus of "Get Me to the Church on Time."**)

HECUBA. Cassandra, thank the Gods.

CASSANDRA. Mother, crown my hair with flowers of war.
We're winning! That's what the blood star sings.
Look at him! Mars is winking at us.
Troy's his meat and drink –
– we're dripping down his chin
Like melted lard.
A blood-red eye in the sky
A Cyclops in love with disaster –
I'm so happy I could die.

HECUBA. Please. I need to ask you / something darling –

CASSANDRA. I will die! We all will.
Cities die, and take us with them.
Why is that such a problem?

HECUBA. Cassandra, where's Polly X?

CASSANDRA. She's around. You're showing the symptoms of depression. Or post-partum something or other.
What's that syndrome you get after your children die?

HECUBA. Oh, let me search in the sand. It's swallowed all my boys.

(**HECUBA** *lies in the dirt as* **MICA** *enters. He has a clipboard and addresses the audience directly – who are townspeople outside the camp perimeter, waiting to know their fate. Perhaps they are ghosts.*)

MICA. Friends, Allies, Townspeople.
What is the strategic plan for Troy? – You may well ask.
To think of "Troy" as a failed state, mired in civil war and ancient hatreds, is to take an unnecessarily negative view. We must look to the future. We must imagine Troy rebuilding itself over the bones and rubble of the past! Pulling itself back up by the crutches. I mean, by the bootstraps. – Any questions?

---

* Please see Music Use Note on Page 3.

MICA. *(cont.)* – Any English speakers out there today?
    (beat)
    They tell you you'll see the world.
    They put you in sealed planes
    and tell you you're traveling,
    but somehow you always end up in Troy.

CASSANDRA. I know. When does a place become a ruin?
    Does someone actually have to ruin it, like they've
    done here?
    Is / history a tide?

MICA. – History?
    That's why we have museums.

CASSANDRA. Or is it a machine? Organic – or invented?
    Can a machine get pregnant?
    I need to know these things.
    The starting data affects my precognition.

HECUBA. Cassandra, please.

CASSANDRA. You never listen, Mama. I want to be a biolo-
    gist of history.

    (CASSANDRA *sings the first two lines of the chorus of "Get
    Me to the Church on Time."**)

MICA. You! No singing outside the tents. *(returns to his cap-
    tive audience)*
    Well, you see a lot. It's not a bad life.
    "Join the world and see the army!"
    I mean…the world. I mean…
    (seeing HELEN*)* Wow.

    (HELEN *sweeps on in make-up and in high heels. She
    holds a movie star pose in her own pink spotlight. We
    ache for the cigarette she doesn't have. The camp lights
    go on; the worlds come together.* MICA *is transfixed.*)

    (ESME *and* CLEA *enter, in* HELEN*'s wake.*)

---

* Please see Music Use Note on Page 3.

HELEN. Does anyone have any Tylenol?

CLEA. *(aside to* **ESME***)* Here we go.

HELEN. *(turning to* **MICA***)* I wonder if you could possibly…?

MICA. Sorry, we only have supplies for our own forces.

*(***HELEN*** looks at him.)*

MICA. But um – well, let's see.

(He dashes off to hunt for Tylenol.)

HELEN. Does anyone have any Perrier? The tank water tastes vile.

CLEA. She wants a drink, ladies.

ESME. It's thirsty work, Helen. Destroying a city.

HELEN. Oh *please.*

CLEA. Yeah, no wonder she needs a drink.

ESME. I need a drink.

HELEN. I suppose you like drinking mud. Since you're wallowing in it. I prefer water.

ESME. Yeah, you want to keep your skin hydrated.

CLEA. Basic maintenance for you –

ESME. – Like keeping your gun oiled.

HELEN. That's right, blame the foreigner. You are such fucking losers. Jealousy is very unbecoming in women.

CLEA. And in men? Lethal.

ESME. *(conversationally, to* **CLEA***)* Speaking of drinking. I saw a little girl on the road here. She was crying because she was burned all over from that stuff –

ESME & CLEA. that's not napalm.

ESME. – We're supposed to keep walking, right, and not talk to the soldiers, but her mother falls at a soldier's feet and begs for water. This soldier is a young guy, fresh off the plane, buzz-cut, pink neck. He signals his commander and the guy says, "No deal, we only have supplies –

ESME & CLEA. – "for our *own forces.*"

HELEN. Your point is, exactly?

HECUBA. *(stirring from the dirt)* Ah, there you are. The face that torched a thousand lives.

HELEN. Oh, you've woken up.

Well, I bow to you. You are the expert.

Nobody does suffering better than you.

HECUBA. And no-one unleashes it with cleaner hands than yours.

HELEN. Really.

Well, I ask you all.

This Wailing Women routine:

We're in a camp. For *just women.*

Ergo, we will be dealing with men.

And if I might point out from my fairly extensive experience:

You'd do a lot better with a smile on your face and a dab of lipstick.

– Just a suggestion.

CASSANDRA. I fucked a horse.

HECUBA. Cassandra, please.

CASSANDRA. I fucked a sea horse with a foaming mane.
It must have been Apollo.

HELEN. Why do I bother.

HECUBA. My poor darling girl. What will they do with you?

(MICA returns bearing gifts.)

ESME. *(referring to MICA and HELEN)* Here we go.

CASSANDRA. There's nothing wrong with me.

Relatively speaking.

I loved a god. I didn't start a war.

MICA. Back home we love God too.

HELEN. And we don't hold grudges.

ESME & CLEA. Right.

MICA. Right! We barely remember our former enemies.

CASSANDRA. Forgotten, but not gone.

HELEN. *(to MICA)* I'd remember you.

MICA. *(to* **HELEN***)* You're unforgettable.

ESME. He's got a point there.

CLEA. Yeah.

HELEN. *(to* **MICA***)* You see what I have to put up with! They don't like foreigners! My head is splitting. Do you think…just two little Tylenol?

MICA. Don't tell anyone.

(**MICA** *surreptitiously hands* **HELEN** *the Tylenol, and a little cup of water.*)

HELEN. *(to the entire world)* Now, that's what I call Civilized –

ESME. – We've noticed.

HELEN. – It's not all revenge, revenge, revenge. So you date one guy on Tuesday and another on Friday and there's not a fucking war about it for the next ten years.

MICA. Right.

HELEN. You inhabit the present.

CASSANDRA. The present is pregnant with death.

Because the past fucked it already.

HELEN. For God's sake, lighten up, Cassandra.

Everything round here stinks like a fish in the sun.

It's old. It's rotten. It's all over except the re-runs.

CASSANDRA. I just said that already.

(**HELEN** *sweeps out, followed by* **MICA**. **TALTHYBIUS** *enters.* **CLEA** *and* **ESME** *leave, sensing trouble.*)

TALTHYBIUS. *(to* **HECUBA***)* Madam.

CASSANDRA. *(to* **TALTHYBIUS***)* I fucked a horse. He was a lot bigger than you.

(**CASSANDRA** *canters and dances lasciviously about the stage during the following.* **TALTHYBIUS** *keeps a wary eye on her.*)

TALTHYBIUS. Madam. I think you remember me.

HECUBA. From better times. It's not good news, is it?

TALTHYBIUS. Well. That's the thing. There are two ways of looking at it. The glass is half-empty or it's half-full, I guess.

HECUBA. I used to complain that no-one ever reported the news from Troy. The world ignored us. But my Serbian friends used to say, if you're not in the news, rejoice. Because every time we're in the world news, it's very bad news indeed. So.

TALTHYBIUS. Just think, Madam, in gentler times…

HECUBA. I don't think so, Talthybius.

(**CASSANDRA** *makes horsey noises and obscene movements.*)

TALTHYBIUS. I need to speak with you privately.

HECUBA. What is it?

TALTHYBIUS. Madam. We are all called upon to make sacrifices.

HECUBA. Spit it out, goddamn you. Where is my Polly X?

TALTHYBIUS. Polly X is…taken care of. Her problems are over; she's – she'll be an attendant.

In the Achilles museum gift shop.

HECUBA. Talthybius, I should like to see her.

TALTHYBIUS. First, Madam, we need to discuss Cassandra.

CASSANDRA. I can taste blood on my tongue. That means the future's being born.

It's trying to come up through my mouth.

HECUBA. No. NOOOOO! Not my Cassandra. Don't take her too! Aaaaiiiiiiieeeee!

TALTHYBIUS. Madam. Please, Madam, compose yourself. *(aside)* Shit of a job. *(beat)*

I will give Cassandra time to prepare.

CASSANDRA. *(sane and deadly)* Oh, I'll be ready. Don't you worry.

Scene Three

(**LOTTE** *appears high above the camp in a dim light, as if in the far distance of* **CASSANDRA***'s prescient vision. She is a little flustered, trying to get her bearings. She has a small practical travel roll-on suitcase. She is finding her way from the first [wrong] hotel, to the assigned hotel one block away. She has an inconveniently-sized fold-out map, which she consults several times before seeing the welcoming pink sign:* Claude's Cultural Oasis. *She makes towards it with purpose.*)

Scene Four

*(POLLY is sharing a bottle of beer with JORGE and MAX.
She is drunk on three sips and feeling sophisticated and
daring. They are in the zoo, at the cage of the tigers.
There are several yellow bottle-tops strewn around them.)*

POLLY X. Gimme that.

MAX. Nope. You've had enough.

JORGE. Little girls shouldn't drink.

MAX. Good girls don't drink.

POLLY X. Yeah, but I'm bad. – Weren't you supposed to be
taking me somewhere?
To meet Achilles' ghost or go to a sacrifice or something? *(She giggles.)*

JORGE. Quick detour.

MAX. We are somewhere, honey. The Zoo.

JORGE. No point in rushing. Achilles' ghost can stay thirsty
a bit longer.

MAX. Speaking of thirsty –

(MAX reaches for another beer.)

POLLY X. Ghosts don't get thirsty.

JORGE. You wish.

POLLY X. I don't care.

MAX. But you will.

JORGE. Shut up, Max. Let the girl have a drink.

(MAX holds the beer out to her.)

MAX. So, *how* bad are you?

POLLY X. Very.

MAX. I'll hold you to that.

(He passes her the beer.)

POLLY X. *(to JORGE)* Do you like Modern Sculpture?

JORGE. Sure.

POLLY X. All of it?

JORGE. What's not to like?

POLLY X. The stuff that's ripped up and shit like that. Like a house inside a rat with fat yellow eyes. And blood coming out the bottom. Stuff like that, that no-one even wants to loot.

(beat)

JORGE. What's not to like?

(They look at the tigers.)

MAX. That's a fucking pussy cat, not a tiger. Call that a tiger, there's bigger tigers than that in Las Vegas.

POLLY X. I wanna go there!

JORGE. You gotta die first.

POLLY X. Why?

MAX. Because, Princess, Las Vegas is Heaven. You only go there when you're dead.

JORGE. Or un-dead. Like Elvis. That's where Buffy the Vampire Slayer's going to end up.

POLLY X. Actually I *am* a princess. If you cut me, you'll get oil on you, we're that rich.

JORGE. Not any more.

POLLY X. That was mean.

MAX. Yes it was. – Tonight you get to do everything you ever wanted to.

POLLY X. How come?

JORGE. Because ghosts are fucking assholes.

MAX. Because this is your party. Who knows, it could last three thousand years.

POLLY X. Oh great, so we'll drink flat beer and look at sad tigers. Why are we in the zoo?

JORGE. The only place away from barracks where you can have a beer without getting shot at.

POLLY X. That's soooo brilliant!

MAX. We both thought of it.

(beat)

POLLY X. *(to* **JORGE***)* I'm going to be an artist and do Modern Sculpture. Have you got any tattoos?

JORGE. Maybe.

POLLY X. Why are the tigers so sad?

JORGE. Combat stress.

POLLY X. His fur's all falling out.

JORGE. Yeah.

POLLY X. C'mon, show me your tatts.

JORGE. Later!

(He opens another beer for her. Another yellow beer bottle top hits the ground.)

POLLY X. Hey! Don't litter.

(She picks up the beer bottle top.)

POLLY X. I'm going to make something with these.

JORGE. Yeah, like what?

POLLY X. Like a sculpture.

JORGE & MAX. A sculpture.

(They clink bottles.)

Scene Five

*(**LOTTE** sits under a bright umbrella, writing a post-card, and sips frozen lemonade mixed with ouzo. She is a bit tipsy and has had a lot of sun.)*

LOTTE. "Dear Auntie Flora,

I'm so glad you hassled me to get out of my rut. The light here is really beautiful, and the people aren't all dreadful." *(revising)* … "the people are really very nice."

(to herself)

Well, some of them.

Well, Clive.

He doesn't say much but I think he has a Past.

You don't want to pry of course.

The other day he asked me if I had "known sorrow." It was such – it took me aback because it was such an odd way to put it. Not, are you sad, but have you – I fudged it of course and laughed and said well, you make the best of things, you move on –

Ah, he said. Just like that. 'Ah'. I felt so shallow.

But the next day was better, I was almost relaxed. Well, all the tour groups go to the same places every day, and you can't talk about relics all the time can you. It's so dusty and dry here. History's fascinating – but bits of it stick in your throat and after a few hours, more than anything you just want a cool lemonade in one of those little Turkish cafes. It's so easy to get dehydrated. And *lost*, my God.

Speaking of thirsty. Just yesterday we were walking round in circles trying to find the Delphic Oracle, but it's confusing because there's Athena's shrine and the Gallipoli exhibit and half the signs are in Turkish. Anyway Clive and I got separated from the tour group and we were completely lost in *minutes*. We were absolutely parched, but the place was like a morgue – do they have siestas here? Not a fly moving – and the sea still as granite. It really could have been 5000 BCE.

LOTTE. *(cont.)* Finally after about *three centuries* we found a little girl, selling lemonade in just her underpants. She could hardly lift up the jug, she was so little. Of course it was luke-warm and sugary but at the time, honestly, it was pure ambrosia!

You know – it actually *is* a great way to meet people. At first you think, a cultural tour for singles, how dreary, how forced…

(CLIVE obligingly appears in LOTTE's daydream, looking handsome and grave in a pink suit.)

But after that kind of day, I think I could quite legitimately join Clive for a sunset glass of Sangria – conversation seems to flow more easily here than back at home. "The dusk in Turkey is really quite stunning" "Yes, and especially at this time of year" "Oh, have you visited in Winter"? – that kind of thing. And I'm sure in just a few days it will seem only natural, because you're in Europe – sort of – to take a little stroll together before dinner –

(CLIVE takes LOTTE's arm, bowing slightly, and they stroll.)

– and anyway the dead can stay dead, because history's all around us, in a shopworn and dusty silence, and perhaps it's the wine, but it seems sad and quite lovely all at the same time, that you have to carve this space out of your schedule and pay thousands of pounds, and come all this way, just to walk slowly through the olive trees beside a nice man at sunset –

(ANDROMACHE enters LOTTE's space, clutching a doll boy. She is elegantly dressed, upper-class, but her clothes are ripped, her shoes gone. ANDROMACHE barely registers LOTTE; she is in shock.)

ANDROMACHE. Where am I?

LOTTE. *(jolted rudely from her reverie)* Pardon?

(In the unkind light, we see that CLIVE is actually the waiter.)

CLIVE. Do you need change, Ma'am?

LOTTE. Uh – no. No. Thank you.

(**CLIVE** *leaves.*)

ANDROMACHE. Where am I? I've been walking for ages and ages. Round in circles.

LOTTE. This is about a mile from the main bus station. Have you lost your tour group? I was wandering around myself yesterday/ for many hours...

ANDROMACHE. The bridges are all burning. I saw a soldier drag a boy, he must have only been ten, into an alley and beat him to death with a rifle butt. They painted red crosses on every door, and then shot up the houses. With people in them. A soldier came into the palace and shat on the carpet. The peacocks – all beheaded. The horses let loose, then shot and left for the vultures. – What makes someone do that? Do they think the horses hate them?

LOTTE. (*at a complete loss*) I don't know. That sounds terrible. Are you sure you're all right?

ANDROMACHE. Well. The city's been torched. My husband's gone. The women –

LOTTE. Perhaps you should sit down. Would you like some water?

(**ANDROMACHE** *takes the water, and drinks the bottle in one gulp.*)

LOTTE. You really have to be careful not to get dehydrated. It's terribly easy. Why, just the other day we were wandering around for *ages* / until we found...

ANDROMACHE. My broken city. Raped by the sword and flame. Ash and dust your shroud.

(*beat*)

LOTTE. It is sad, to think of the city being obliterated so many times. But on the other hand, if it wasn't, it wouldn't have got into history, would it, and we wouldn't be here.

ANDROMACHE. My mother in law said the same:

> *We sacrificed for nothing. And yet,*
> *had the gods not cursed this city and crushed us to dust and*
> *ruin,*
> *we should have vanished into darkness*
> *and left no theme for poets*
> *and the men yet to be born.*

LOTTE. *(deflated)* Well. She said it much better than me.

I mean no-one writes about ordinary boring places, like Reading back home.

You really are lost, aren't you?

What a precious little doll. And in such good condition!

Where did/ you get him?

ANDROMACHE. My son is all I have left.

LOTTE. Oh.

Well, some people never get children in the first place. Or husbands. – Though I do see a lot of children through my work. We repair dolls, you see, and we have "visiting hours" just like at a real hospital. The older ones can watch if they want. The younger ones get too upset, they think the dolls are alive, bless them…

But you know, the crazy thing is, once you've spent thirty hours on a doll, you do come to feel that she's alive, or – not exactly alive, but – latent, do you know what I mean?

Sort of potentially alive, because they always might become somebody, whereas we actually are, and that's inevitably disappointing. You tick off, one by one, all the things that don't seem likely to happen any more: A child. Finding a man without serious Issues, or an ex-wife and custody problems. Affording an apartment in London, even an hour out East. A life in another country.

ANDROMACHE. There is no life in another country. You'll always be a foreigner, stuck on the wrong side of the looking-glass. – I just don't understand. I did everything right. I ironed Hector's shirts. I stayed home and cooked. I didn't sleep around.

LOTTE. Listen, it happens. I've been through it myself. What was it, a younger woman?

ANDROMACHE. When he got upset about our reading group, I stopped going. I didn't go out on my own at night, even when he was away for months. Talk is a poisonous thing. I looked down when he spoke to me. I reserved those moments when I imposed my own will, for the really important things. And now that bitch from Hell, who has never obeyed anything but her own desires, has destroyed everything. I sometimes think she really must be immortal. Because she has an inhuman – a god-like – incapacity for remorse.
The world revolves around her, and if bits of it fall off – well, too bad.

LOTTE. I understand how you feel. But I think if she's as shallow as all that, one day your husband will realize what he's lost. And no-one stays young and beautiful forever.

ANDROMACHE. My husband is dead. And you obviously don't know Helen.

(*MICA enters.*)

MICA. I told you, stay within the perimeter fence.

(*MICA starts to drag* **ANDROMACHE** *roughly away.*)

LOTTE. Hey. Hey! That's not OK! She was just lost! (*calling after* **ANDROMACHE**) You should complain! In writing!

MICA. You too, Miss. Move!

(*MICA grabs* **LOTTE** *and drags both of the women along.*)

LOTTE. Hey. HEY! Get your hands off me. I'm not in your tour group. Police!

(*MICA backhands her and drags the women away. As if summoned by the violence of the slap,* **CASSANDRA** *suddenly appears in the space of the Gods. She watches the women and* **MICA** *leave.*)

Scene Six

CASSANDRA. I think history's a wave. I think that's it.
It rolls and sucks at you and drags you under.
It smashes you into the future
right when you think you're on solid ground.
Like stepping on a landmine.

I like riding that wave. I like plunging my face in its
foam.

I stole my horse from the sea
My Apollo –
he was drowning! I'm on the shore
watching him struggle – I know
the water's freezing
Too cold to survive
but there's a strong cord,
a cord like love
only darker, tying me to him
so I swim out to him
plunge my hands in his mane
drag him back to the shore. He sinks
to his knees
in the shallows and we're both
frozen – his heart's shuddering
like my teeth –

but then he bites me,
he won't let me go,
he gets over me and bites me
with his teeth on my neck
and nuzzles me with his soft
velvet mouth and then
he pushes his huge hot horse's cock into me
and I start to warm up....

and then we're fucking
on the shoreline
where the waves churn into wet sand
and I'm crying because
I want to turn into foam
but I
want
him
more.
'Cause he's pointing a gun at me
and I'm moaning and pulling on the trigger.

(beat)

And since then my belly has felt hot inside
like it's full of snakes. Something's growing in there.
Sometimes I hear the click of metal
when I walk
or the rasping of steel.

I think –
I think I'm pregnant with guns and bombs.
And the first man I'm with,
soon as he's in me –
that's it.
The world's going to blow.

I'm so happy I could die.

(She sings the first two lines of the chorus of "Get Me to the Church on Time.")

---

*Please see Music Use Note on Page Three

Scene Seven

*(Back at the zoo. The ground is strewn with yellow beer bottle tops. **POLLY X** is making a necklace out of beer bottle tops. The men aren't listening to **POLLY**'s chatter, at least not to begin with.)*

POLLY X. – And then after Paris and traveling round the world I'm going to be a famous sculptor and have an exhibition in the zoo! I'm doing tigers and Barbies...

JORGE. What's he's thinking about?

MAX. Who?

JORGE. The tiger.

POLLY X. ...and I'm calling it CAGE RAGE!

MAX. Oh. Old Mr. Stripey.

POLLY X. You guys / are cool –

JORGE. Yeah –

POLLY X. – You haven't got those gross pink / necks.

JORGE. – What's he thinking?

MAX. About meat. Same as / us.

POLLY X. And you're not fat –

JORGE. – C'mon, he's a tiger.

POLLY X. – not like a lot of the soldiers.

JORGE. – Can't just be meat on his mind, that's boring.

MAX. Not if you're hungry.

POLLY X. I'm getting hungry.

MAX. Me too, Princess.

JORGE. I bet he's planning something.

MAX. Yeah, planning the hunt.

POLLY X. He's half bald.

MAX. *(to **POLLY X**)* Sign of virility.

JORGE. Bullshit. – I bet he's thinking about escape.

MAX. Where would he go?

JORGE. Good point.

MAX. If he escaped, he'd just get shot anyway.

POLLY X. I like beer.

(Beat. The men shift their attention to **POLLY X.***)*

POLLY X. I hate the camp. It's boring and everyone just lies around and cries. My mama cut all her hair off and put it on the graves of the other kids. She looks like a vulture now. She never even talks to me, I don't think she sees me; she just looks straight through me then lies back down in the dirt. It's awful.

MAX. You should see our tents.

JORGE. You should smell our tents.

POLLY X. She used to be really like, "Wash your hands" and "What if you had an accident and you hadn't changed your knickers?" Now, she's just completely let herself go. I stuck a safety pin through my eyebrow and she didn't even notice. And before, she wouldn't even let me get my ears pierced!!! It's like she's a ghost – or even worse – like *I'm* a ghost, like I'm dead already. Don't make me go back, OK? OK?

JORGE. Don't worry, you're not going back.

POLLY X. I'm *not* going back. – Gimme that.

MAX. Come here and ask nicely, Princess.

*(***POLLY*** tries to grab the beer, giggling.* **MAX** *grabs her and sits her on his lap, holds it out of reach.)*

MAX. Come n' get it.

POLLY X. I can't reach. Jorge, help me! Please….

MAX. Undo your shirt.

POLLY X. What? No way. Why?

MAX. 'Cause then you'll get a drink.

JORGE. Come on, man.

*(***JORGE*** takes the beer from* **MAX** *and hands it to* **POLLY X.***)*

MAX. What's wrong with you? We're just fooling around.

(beat)

JORGE. Ever seen how they train tigers?

(POLLY X moves over to JORGE.)

MAX. He's a strange guy, Princess. You should stick with real men.

POLLY X. I don't know any. *(to JORGE)* How do they train tigers, Mr. Soldier?

JORGE. Tigers are just big pussy cats, after all. They take a long time just to get used to you. So you got to do two things. First one is get them used to you. You don't make any sudden moves at first. You show up the same time every day and do exactly the same things.

POLLY X. Like what?

JORGE. Like…. this.

(He holds the beer for her, gently and seductively tipping it into her mouth.)

POLLY X. But I'm a girl.

MAX. You sure are, Princess.

JORGE. I'm just showing you, see. And then when you've got them all feeling relaxed, you surprise them. Show them who's boss.

POLLY X. That doesn't sound hard.

(JORGE puts the beer down carefully. Then quickly twists POLLY's arm behind her back so she's suddenly kneeling on the ground in front of him.)

POLLY X. Ow! Ow, for real!

JORGE. Undo your shirt.

(POLLY starts to undo her shirt.)

MAX. Yeah, that's it babe.

JORGE. Shut up, Max.

POLLY X. *(snapping out of it)* Yeah, shut up Max.

(She buttons her shirt back up, in a very Princess way. JORGE laughs at her.)

POLLY X. What?

JORGE. You're such a little kid.

POLLY X. I am not.

(She slides back onto his lap.)

POLLY X. Tell me more about tigers.

JORGE. Well, tigers do best with one trainer. Or else they get confused.

(MAX moves behind her and tries to kiss her neck.)

POLLY X. Hey! Stop that.

JORGE. Lighten up, Princess. It's a party.

POLLY X. I don't like it.

MAX. You're lucky it's us and not the Marines.

JORGE. He's right about that.

POLLY X. *(softly, to JORGE)* I like you.

(beat)

JORGE. Ah, shit. Take it easy, Max.

MAX. Come on man. Fourteen fucking weeks straight of Operation Intensive Bullshit. Just a little bit of fun. She's finished anyway. You know that.

POLLY X. I am not. I can hold my beer.

JORGE. There's worse ways to go than dead drunk.

POLLY X. I don't feel so good.

JORGE. Dizzy?

POLLY X. Mmm –hmm.

JORGE. *(sitting her down)* Just lean back and relax. And close your eyes. You'll be OK.

MAX. Mmmm, Princess.

JORGE. See, no-one's going to hurt you.

POLLY X. OK.

JORGE. *(softly)* I like you too, Princess. You're a good girl.

MAX. Yeah. Too good to fucking waste on a dead man. Come on –

(MAX tries to lift POLLY off JORGE's knees. POLLY is promptly, violently sick.)

MAX. Shit! Shit!

(He drops her. She is on all fours, vomiting. **JORGE** *laughs, and laughs too much.)*

I hate this fucking country! Everything you touch turns to shit!

(Sound of tigers roaring. Lights.)

Scene Eight

(Back in the camp.)

CLEA. Esme. Do you know where we'll be going?

ESME. Or will they just kill us in the tent?

CLEA. I guess we're prostitutes, now.

ESME. I doubt it. We won't be getting paid.

CLEA. Or ghosts in the dead zone at immigration. I heard about this Iranian guy, he'd been living in Charles de Gaulle airport for fourteen years. Got his papers cleared to escape to Paris, but then they wouldn't grant him asylum. So he's allowed to land, see, but not to leave. Can't go forwards and he can't go back. Finally topped himself in the men's toilets near the International Food Court in Arrivals.

ESME. There's a black hole now, where I used to think "future."

OK, not such a great future, but something you could stitch together

out of family, language, shared jokes, even going hungry.

But now

it's like someone tore up a map

and that map was my body.

CLEA. There's a country without borders

growing like an oil spill.

A space where you can't live –

ESME. – but you can't, strictly speaking, die.

CLEA & ESME. That's our new home.

Charles de Gaulle airport all over the world.

CLEA. We don't belong anywhere.

ESME. Not since our city burned –

CLEA & ESME. and the flags all got torn up for bandages.

HECUBA. Flags are always bandages. They end up like us:
memory wrapped round a corpse.
Maybe some General in uniform
will bestow one on an Argive woman
who's just lost her son killing our husbands.
How obscenely light it feels in her lap.

HECUBA, CLEA, ESME. To lose a son and gain a flag.

HECUBA. I don't think most women are so stupid
as to see that as a bargain

HECUBA, CLEA, ESME. no matter where they live.

(**TALYTHYBIUS** enters.)

TALTHYBIUS. Madam.

HECUBA. What now? The Bad News Bird, here to pick out
the next corpse.

TALYTHYBIUS. Madam, just think, in another time, we
might have been friends.

HECUBA. Your wife must tear you to pieces if you think of
me as your friend.

ESME. All his friends have beaks –

CLEA. – And claws –

CLEA & ESME. – And bald heads.

TALTHYBIUS. I was just trying to suggest that often, people
are better than their circumstances. That we do things
not because we want to, but because we happen to
have a talent for say, languages, instead of physics or
radar, and then you end up having to talk to people
whom you only meet when your country has invaded
theirs. All I am trying / to say –

HECUBA. – is that you let yourself be used by murderers,
against your better judgment. It's not impressive. So,
spit it out, whatever vile tidbit of news you've got in
your beak. It stinks; I can smell it from here.

TALTHYBIUS. If that's the way you want it. Your mad daughter is coming with me. It's an honor for her, to marry
a General.

HECUBA. She's really not the marrying kind.

ESME. She prefers horses –

CLEA. Yeah, big ones –

ESME & CLEA. – We know about you.

TALTHYBIUS. The General likes crazy bitches. He's taking her home on a leash.

CLEA. What about us? Where are we going?

TALTHYBIUS. I'm still sorting out the ruling family.

(A flashlight flickers from inside the tent walls. There's the loud thunk of the power being switched off. Then the camp lights go out, leaving an eerie half-light, like the orange glow of a city glimpsed at night from the freeway.)

TALTHYBIUS. Are they trying to blow up the generator? Stop that!

(TALTHYBIUS runs off to investigate. CASSANDRA the saboteur steals out, flashlight in hand.)

CASSANDRA. I knew it. Didn't I, mother?
I'm marrying disaster!
Soon as he's in me we're gone
Washed in a bloody tide –
Bring flowers for the bridegroom
And medals for the bride!

HECUBA. Cassie, please. Let me hold you.

CASSANDRA. Don't you worry about The Boss, Mama:
He's got a bad trip home.
There's a huge monster with one eye
and a taste for sailors and lamb fat.
Singing ladies on the rocks
And half-men, half-horses
with enormous muscles/ and HUGE COCKS –

HECUBA. Darling, please do try to stop thinking about horses.

(TALTHYBIUS returns as the camp lights clunk back on.)

TALTHYBIUS. I don't get it. All this *(gesturing to* **ESME** *and* **CLEA***)* and he chooses her.

CASSANDRA. You're not even worth spitting on, you tyrant's asswipe.

TALTHYBIUS. I hope the General finds a way to shut your mouth while having his pleasure.

(to **HECUBA***)* Madam –

*(***TALTHYBIUS** *drags* **CASSANDRA** *away. She sings an idiot song as she goes, which is abruptly silenced at some point offstage as* **TALTHYBIUS** *gags her.)*

CASSANDRA. *(singing)* Goodbye Mama

Don't be sad.

I'll kill our enemies for you and Dad.

You'll be so proud

I'll sing aloud

We'll meet again Below

I'll have a string of skulls with me

And bloody hands to show –

A family dismembered

all dancing in a row.

HECUBA. So. I married a king.

I bore children.

All gone now.

Salt on my tongue –

The buzzing taste of blood.

I lick the bitter iron blade of murder

On my knees – On my knees.

*(***MICA** *enters with his prisoners,* **ANDROMACHE** *and* **LOTTE***, and flings them into the camp.)*

MICA. And stay there! All of you! I've been very patient. But the next bitch I find wandering around gets shot.

*(***MICA** *exits.)*

HECUBA. Andromache!

*(***ANDROMACHE** *moves to* **HECUBA***. They embrace. The women ignore* **LOTTE***.)*

LOTTE. This is a clear breach of human rights. Who set up this camp? I want to speak / to the Embassy!

ANDROMACHE. Enslaved, now –

HECUBA, ESME, CLEA. the whole city, then –

ANDROMACHE. Only my son left –

HECUBA. My children –

ANDROMACHE. My husband –

CLEA, ESME, HECUBA. All gone, cut to pieces, drowned or burned –

LOTTE. Excuse me –

CLEA. – From that stuff that's not napalm

ESME. Smart bombs

CLEA. Shrapnel

CLEA & ESME. Spent uranium

ANDROMACHE. Given the gun's farewell.

LOTTE. Excuse me / I wonder if....

HECUBA, CLEA, ESME. Our young men sprawled at the city walls

ANDROMACHE. A feast for rats

HECUBA, CLEA, ESME. While Troy puts on collar and chain.

(*HECUBA and* **ANDROMACHE,** *comforting one another, move behind the scrim with* **ESME** *and* **CLEA.**)

LOTTE. Who is in charge here???

(**HELEN** *emerges dramatically, having spied* **LOTTE**'s *useful pocketbook.*)

HELEN. Welcome To The Dark Ages.

LOTTE. Oh, thank God. – I'm Lotte. Lotte Jones. And... you look familiar. Are you...?

HELEN. Helen. (*beat*) Just Helen.

LOTTE. So who is in charge here? I need to / find out...

HELEN. There's no point, you know.

LOTTE. Well, I think –

HELEN. They don't listen to anyone. They are soooo determined to have their Tragedy.

LOTTE. It's probably PTSD.

HELEN. What?

LOTTE. Post-Traumatic Stress Disorder.

HELEN. Oh, *please*. It's all an act with them. – Oh, is that aspirin in that little bottle?

LOTTE. Yes, I'm down to my last supplies...

(**HELEN** *takes a couple*.)

LOTTE. God, emergency numbers!!

(**LOTTE** *tries to get life out of her cell phone*.)

Hello? The British Embassy, please. Hello.... Hello? – Shit.

HELEN. May I? *(snatching the phone)*

– Hello, Commander in Chief please...What do you mean, who is this? It is his *wife*.... There's no need to be like that.... I'll call back.

(to **LOTTE***)* My husband, Menelaus. He always used to do this.

Get some awful lackey to answer the phone so he can pretend to be busy. It's a typical male power play.

(**HELEN** *throws the phone back to* **LOTTE** *dismissively*).

LOTTE. Hey, be careful! That could very well be our lifeline.

HELEN. Go to hell.

(The phone rings. **HELEN** *grabs it.)*

HELEN. Darling! At last! There's been a terrible misunderstanding and I am dying to see you... Ten years is far too long... Good, then we can talk...Here...Tonight? I've missed you so very much...

(**MENELAUS** *hangs up*.)

– Hello? – Oh. These important men. Always in a hurry. Well – I'd better spruce up for the visit.

(**HELEN** *attempts to leave with* **LOTTE***'s cell phone*.)

LOTTE. Excuse me!

(**HELEN** *returns* **LOTTE***'s phone with bad grace. Beat.*)

HELEN. You know, Lotte, that's one thing *they* just can't get through their heads. *You've* got a nice outfit, decent haircut; you've made the best of a, well, a modest package. But look at them! They're not even all old.

(A ballad begins to play softly. It's like the icky moment in a musical when All Is Lost but the characters pick up their spirits anyway.)

HELEN. If *I* was running the camp, we'd have hot showers and decent meals by now, and probably some nice times in the evenings. Some café tables, with umbrellas, and drinks with umbrellas in them too, and gentlemen callers with cigars. All we ever get now is that African vulture bringing bad news. We'd have some dancing, and those nice strings of holiday lights around the tents – the plain lights, not the colored ones, which are vulgar and passé. It doesn't have to be like this.

LOTTE. *(swept up in* **HELEN***'s rose-colored mood)* I must say, the best part about travel is the enterprising people you meet. Long after you forget all the discomfort and the sunburn and even quite nasty experiences like being kidnapped, it's the conversations and the moments of beauty that really / stay with you.

HELEN. And this all could happen so easily, just by putting a little effort into…well, it's just another form of hospitality. It's what women do, no point moaning about it and just giving up like *they* do.

LOTTE. Yes, you make the best of things –

HELEN. – But they just won't listen.

(Beat. Ballad stops.)

HELEN. You know – I really don't feel accepted here, not even after all these years. They don't take to foreigners. It's a Revenge Culture, you know. Very primordial. If they don't like you…. *(mimes slitting throat)*

LOTTE. Really?

HELEN. Yes!!! *(conspiratorially)* You must be careful. Don't talk to anyone. They have all these secret lines in the sand and if you cross them – even by accident – they'll

HELEN. *(cont.)* never forgive you. And then you could end
up in a ditch and never even know what you've done
wrong.

LOTTE. Good God. Surely it's not that bad.

HELEN. Yes!! You wouldn't believe what I've gone through
here. Don't trust anyone else, Lotte. *(whispering)* I have
a plan – but I've said too much already.

LOTTE. No, please! A plan – What / can I do?

HELEN. Shhh! Stay close. Work on supplies. Stay away from
Them. And Lotte. Whatever you do, don't let yourself
go. – We shouldn't be seen talking.

*(**HELEN** sweeps off, taking **LOTTE**'s nail-polish, hand
sanitizer, and sun-block.)*

LOTTE. Hey, my nail-polish. Hey! *(to **HELEN**'s disappearing
back)* Excuse me – Helen? Excuse me…

*(**LOTTE**'s phone rings. **LOTTE** pounces on it.)*

LOTTE. Hello. Hello…Is anyone out there? Hello?…Hello?

Scene Nine

*(Back at the Zoo. **POLLY X** has passed out on the ground.*
*She wears the bottle-top necklace she has made. **JORGE**'s*
jacket covers her. More beer bottles are strewn around.)

MAX. What is this, day care? Wake her up.

JORGE. No.

MAX. Ah, you're pathetic. Want some action and where do
we end up? In the fucking Zoo! *(to tigers)* Come on you
guys. Show us your teeth! *(He roars. A tiger roars back.)*
Hey, that's more like it! Think they're hungry?

JORGE. Huh?

MAX. We could feed 'em some beef jerky. *(to Tiger)* Hey
Stripey. You hungry?

JORGE. Let's see. There's a war. The locals have to line up
for a bag of rice. His ribs are sticking through his coat.
I'd say – probably – yep. He's hungry.

MAX. You've got a fucking disease, man. Know-it-all-itis.

JORGE. It's the company I keep.

MAX. Hey! We could put the girl in the cage with them!
She could do some dancing! Polly – Wake up! It's
showtime! You're in Vegas!

JORGE. Shut up Max.

MAX. What is your fucking problem? I'm just trying to have
a party. With two corpses and a couple of stuffed animals.

(The tiger roars again.)

MAX. *(to tigers)* Sorry, Stripey. Didn't mean you. *(beat)*
Seriously, man. What are we going to do?

JORGE. Hang out. Get drunk. Deliver the virgin.

MAX. Yeah, twenty-four hours late? They'll have our balls
for breakfast.

JORGE. We'll say we got caught in traffic.

MAX. You're talking out your ass, man. We are gonna pay for tonight, big-time. Might as well get our money's worth. *(pokes* **POLLY** *with his foot)* Come on, wake up! Play time! Mr. Stripey's waiting for you.

POLLY X. Mmmmmmrrrrggggg

MAX. Wake up. I wanna watch you dance. Can you strip?

POLLY X. I feel sick.

JORGE. Leave her alone.

MAX. She's dead. She's dead already!

JORGE. She hasn't even got tits yet.

MAX. She's ready for it. She was all over you.

JORGE. Why don't you feed the tigers. They're "ready for it."

POLLY X. Jorge – I changed my mind. I want to go home.

(*beat*)

JORGE. You said you hated the camp.

POLLY X. Yeah but that's not home.

MAX. Come on, the fun's just starting, Princess.

JORGE. *(to* **MAX***)* Why don't you feed the tigers.

POLLY X. I feel sick.

JORGE. Come here.

(**POLLY** *leans against him. He sponges her face.*)

JORGE. Feel better?

POLLY X. Mmmm.

JORGE. Now watch Uncle Max. He's gonna give the tigers some jerky. Then they'll feel better too.

MAX. Why don't you try it, Princess. They like you.

(*He hands her some jerky.*)

MAX. Army's finest.

(**POLLY** *starts to reach in through the bars.*)

POLLY X. He wanted to bite me!!!

JORGE. He's a tiger. That's what they do, they bite.

MAX. You'll never get to Vegas with an act like that.

You gotta feed them by hand.

Get in the cage, Princess, and show us your stuff.

POLLY X. Only if Jorge comes too. You can get a tiger tattoo for me when I'm dead. Or wear a tooth around your neck or something.

JORGE. No, you hang here with Uncle Max. I know about tigers. I'll go in.

POLLY X. I wanna do it too!

JORGE. In a minute. Let me get them settled. Tigers do best with one trainer.

MAX. He's right, Princess. Let's get cozy and watch, then you can go in once it's safe.

POLLY X. I don't wanna be safe.

MAX. Is that right?

(JORGE *moves towards the cage.* POLLY *grabs his sleeve.*)

POLLY X. Jorge, don't. I changed my mind, all right.

JORGE. Again! – Later.

POLLY X. Let me come too.

MAX. He'll be fine. He's a good soldier. And those tigers are more like stuffed animals.

(JORGE *steps into the tigers' cage, cautiously feeding them.*)

POLLY X. This used to be the best zoo in the whole of the Middle East. We had white tigers and llamas and even a mermaid section. No-one else could keep them alive in captivity.

JORGE. C'mon Mr. Stripey. Not gonna hurt you. Here's dinner.

(to the others) See? Nothing to it. I bet I could get him to roll over.

You wanna see that, Princess?

(MAX *starts fondling* POLLY X, *pushing her against the cage.*)

POLLY X. Stop it! Don't touch me, you fucking barbarian pig! Jorge! Jorge! Help! Jorge!

*(A roar. A scream. **JORGE** curses in Spanish.)*

MAX. Fuck!

*(**MAX** pulls his gun and rushes into the cage. Gunshots. **MAX** and **JORGE** stumble out of the cage; **JORGE**'s arm is badly bitten.)*

POLLY X. You killed them! You murderer!

MAX. Party's over, bitch. MOVE!

*(**MAX** shoves **POLLY** and half-carries **JORGE**. The three stumble off into the darkness.)*

Scene Ten

MICA. As I was saying. We regret any casualties and the loss
of innocent life. Humanitarian priorities are high on
our list. I ask for your patience with the monumental
changes we are installing. Rome wasn't burned in a
day. Built. Rome wasn't built in a day.

Now, progress can be slow. But action isn't everything.
It's being *prepared* for action that matters. Now that
takes discipline, hanging round day after day waiting
for something to happen. The main event here is, the
latrines overflow. That gets pretty exciting. A home
made tattoo gets infected. A bird lands looking for
water. Or someone tries to hang herself in the tent.
Then there's the moaning and wailing. We let that
pass, but we discourage the singing. Singing could
lead to action.

But there's no action.

Any English speakers out there today?
– Fuck.

Well. These long tours of duty, it's all about survival.
Two simple rules:
One: Compartmentalize.
Two: Cover your ass.

For instance, number 1. Managing down time. Well,
there's Helen. Fifty-seven percent of people meet their
partners through work. And I've got a stack of maga-
zines, and I worked out how to link the satellite phone
to the 900 numbers back home. That helps, a little.
Knowing that the World's still out there.

Man, I just can't wait to be back home in Troy, NY.
Walk down to the canal, past that big old statue of
Uncle Sam. Past the old factories and new real estate
offices.

Taste real beer again.

MICA. *(cont.)* Play pool with the guys on Friday and lose half my paycheck. If any of them are still there.

Not much action back home either, with the steelworks finished and half of us enlisted. After ten years away, you're like a ghost, haunting the streets of your own fucking life.

Maybe when I get home I'll just get a big black Humvee with the windows all blacked out. Tear up the map and head West. Drive for three days til I hit the ocean and then just keep on going. Man, I've got so much grit in my eyes they feel like they've been sandpapered. Feel like the whole of the Desert Storm happened right inside my eyeballs. I'm gonna wash them clean with blue, blue water. Let the sand slide away, and the road, and the dry grit that coats your skin and gets in every crack.

I'll just step on the gas and drive into the wide blue smile of the sea.

Helen makes me think of the sea.

And after the first jolt as you hit the water,

everything slows down

real smooth and peaceful.

Fish swim past the windshield.

Maybe a lazy old shark will turn his head to say hello.

Seals. Seaweed.

An old submarine blows bubbles at you from some long-forgotten war,

growing barnacles and leaking poison into the sea.

And slowly you sink down into the green

then the blue

then the inky darkness

where only the giant squids live, blind and harmless.

They won't bother you, and no, they're not winking

it's just a trick of the last little dribble of light.

After a while the barnacles will build a home on the roof.

MICA. *(cont.)* A few more years, and the little fish swim through your eye sockets to hide from the sharks in the back of your skull.

Still "protecting the weak" even here.

– Jesus.

Maybe Helen will move out West with me.

HELEN. *(from camp)* Mica!!

(Hearing HELEN, LOTTE peeps around from the back of the camp to watch. HELEN is aware that LOTTE is watching).

HELEN. Where's that rat-faced guard? *(calling to MICA)* I need some Tylenol. And some soap.

MICA. I'm coming! It'll cost ya, though –

HELEN. *(purring)* Can I put it on credit?

MICA. Sure, honey. I'm keeping count…

HELEN. I bet you are.

MICA. Here you are, honey. Army's finest. Want water with that?

HELEN. Thanks, handsome.

(MICA gives HELEN water and the Tylenol. She drinks.)

MICA. You have the most beautiful neck. When you stretch it up – like a swan. Your Daddy was a swan, wasn't he?

HELEN. Where do you get this superstitious bullshit? Been talking to Them?

MICA. Your beautiful neck inspires these thoughts. Shall we take a little walk?

HELEN. Not now, Napoleon. I told you, I have a headache. And I need to freshen up – *urgently*. Where is the soap you promised?

(MICA hands her the soap; HELEN takes it and grabs the whole bottle of Tylenol too.)

HELEN. – I'll take that, I'm sick of rations.

(She flounces off towards the tents, signaling LOTTE that this is her moment.)

MICA. Shit. *Shit.* Well, Rome wasn't – built – in a day.

(He follows **HELEN***, speaking as he exits.)*

MICA. Helen honey. We need to talk. I'm sorry about your headache. Helen! – I can get sun block. And bubble-bath – Helen! – Beer? I can get champagne! And glasses…

(During the above, a very tense **LOTTE** *creeps out to* **MICA***'s supply pack and starts urgently rifling through.)*

MICA. Hey! Get the fuck away from my cart! *(He runs back on towards her.)*

LOTTE. I just – Water, you/ can get so dehydrated.

MICA. Back away, bitch.

LOTTE. I wasn't trying / to cause any trouble

MICA. Right now. Last warning.

*(***LOTTE** *backs away.)*

Scene Eleven

HECUBA. My city, where I bore my children, all gone.

ANDROMACHE. My boy and I, damaged war loot.

Your son, my poor Hector, can't save us now.

HECUBA. I lost my Cassandra, ripped from my arms right where you stand.

ANDROMACHE. Hecuba. You've lost more than you realize.

HECUBA. That's really not possible.

ANDROMACHE. Polly X is dead. I saw them do it.

They cut your daughter's throat at dawn
at Achilles' grave. Now, they say, the trucks can set off
the sand storm will ease
Achilles' ghost will let them go.

I don't think she felt much when it happened – that's a mercy.
She could hardly stand up straight.
A soldier with a wounded arm held her
She clung to him and had to be prised off.
At the block they paused
to take off the yellow necklace she'd made
from those beer-bottle tops
so the sword could do its job. She gave it to the soldier
and hid her face.
But at the last moment before the sword fell
she tore her shirt open to the waist
stretched up, bare breasted, and shouted:

POLLY X. "See what you're missing out on, corpse-fuckers! TROY RULES!"

*(**POLLY** is suddenly illuminated in the space of the gods, in front of her large pink cardboard heart sculpture, which is now half-finished: it has broken Barbie-dolls nailed to it. She is disheveled and defiant. **JORGE**'s jacket is draped round her shoulders. Through **ANDROMACHE**'s next lines, **POLLY X** and her dolls slowly fade from view.)*

ANDROMACHE. I washed her poor body
and kissed her goodbye for you.
She smelt of beer and clove cigarettes and henna.
The wounded soldier tried to help me.
I didn't let him
but said, If you have any shame, soldier
you'll give me that yellow necklace
for Polly's mother. He refused.
So I spat in his face
which was wet enough already.

HECUBA. To outlive one's children is already to wander
in the world of shades.
Dry water and empty bread
I eat but can't swallow
I hear but can't listen
I dream and I cannot wake up.

Surely
tomorrow morning
there'll be the gentle knock at the door
and my servant will be there
with sweet black tea
for us to drink in bed.
I'll read a few letters –
Polly will bound in and show me her latest sculptures
– which are always hideous –
badly glued bits of junk
but I always say, Lovely,
because I see the need in her
to make something matter.

And then, Priam will wake up and complain
that I've stolen all the blankets, and we won't
turn on the news just yet, no –
we won't
even

HECUBA. *(cont.)* exhale.

> The morning's a sugar cube on our tongues
> we don't move so it won't dissolve.
> Out the window
> the sun is rising, blood red,
> and from the towers
> the call to prayer
> joy in every sun-speck of dust
> in the lines on my husband's face,
> the dirt under my Polly's nails
> from scratching away in junk –
> She's cut herself.
> Oh no, she's cut herself.
>
> What's wrong, what's wrong, my darling?
> – I must have bit my tongue. My mouth is full of blood.

*(**HECUBA** spits. Then weeps.)*

ANDROMACHE. Hecuba, she's better off.

> She's in a place beyond pain now.
> Think about it – for us
> it's worse. What's left for us –
> to pleasure our husbands' murderers?
> I wish I was dead too.

HECUBA. Andromache, it's still better to be alive –

> You still have your son.
>
> There's at least a chance
> that your boy might grow up
> and one day return to Troy
> rebuild the palaces
> bring back the peacocks in the garden
> restore the art museum
> in our Polly's name…
>
> Plant a seed in the ashes
> and grow a forest back.

(*TALTHYBIUS enters.*)

TALTHYBIUS. (*to* HECUBA) Madam.

(*to* ANDROMACHE) Madam.

I had a great deal of respect for your late husband, Hector.

ANDROMACHE. What is it?

TALTHYBIUS. I'm afraid it concerns your child.

ANDROMACHE. Oh no. Please don't separate us. He's too young to be a slave / on his own

TALTHYBIUS. He won't be made a slave. Never.

ANDROMACHE. I'm not leaving him behind – is that what you're suggesting?

TALTHYBIUS. No.

(*beat*)

HECUBA. Spit it out, vulture.

TALTHYBIUS. They will drive over his skull with a tank. On automatic pilot, so no man bears the child's blood on his hands. Then he won't grow up and revenge his family.

HECUBA. What family? What's left?

TALTHYBIUS. There's nothing I can do, I'm sorry.

HECUBA. There never is.

TALTHYBIUS. (*to* ANDROMACHE) Madam – don't fight it. If you hand him over, they'll let you bury him.

I'll bring him back to you for a proper burial. I promise.

HECUBA. I will hold you to that, Talthybius.

ANDROMACHE. Why kill this child? He never did anything to you!

(*She sees* MICA, *behind her with a gun*).

TALTHYBIUS. Alive – or dead?

(ANDROMACHE, *outflanked, hands* TALTHYBIUS *the child and collapses.*)

HECUBA. Talthybius. My whole family lies unburied, under the wreckage of your war. I beg you not to take him.

(beat)

TALTHYBIUS. Madam. I've done all I can.

*(**TALTHYBIUS** turns to leave, but **HECUBA**'s next words bring him pause.)*

HECUBA. Return him for burial then. Or I will hunt you down like a dog. Through the underworld if I have to, blind and drooling, following the scent of your betrayal.

*(**TALTHYBIUS** leaves with the child. **ANDROMACHE** collapses and **HECUBA** holds her. A beat, then **MAX** and **JORGE** enter. **JORGE**'s arm is bandaged.)*

JORGE. *(to **ANDROMACHE**)* Ma'am. We have orders to escort you to the trucks.

MAX. Move it along Ma'am.

ANDROMACHE. We won't see each other again, Hecuba.

HECUBA. No. I'll wash and bury your son, then.

*(**JORGE** and **MAX** start leading **ANDROMACHE** away.)*

ANDROMACHE. This is Polly's Mother, Soldier.

*(**JORGE** pauses.)*

MAX. Come on, man.

*(**JORGE** throws **POLLY**'s yellow bottle top necklace to **HECUBA**.)*

*(Then he, **MAX** and **ANDROMACHE** exit.)*

*(A moment of **HECUBA** alone, holding **POLLY X**'s necklace.)*

Scene Twelve

(**CASSANDRA** *appears in the space of the Gods. Since her capture she has been repeatedly raped. She is disheveled and in a torn and dirty sex outfit.*)

CASSANDRA. Hecuba!
I told you things would work out!
Death comes full circle
To star your neck with hate –
My thighs are wet with it.
I tore his face
And sucked it out of his cock –
I didn't know hate was so juicy.

Forget love. It melts away like useless fat
Under the napalm rain.
What's left of love? Not Polly. Not your grandson.
Some ugly photos of howling women
To wrap the trash in when the news turns stale.

So get up, Mother.
Put on Polly's necklace.
Look, its stars are yellow wounds
Torn in the night's black skin

Bring on Troy's last night –
Her dark wings ring the future:
The only fertile seed is hate
Sown in our guts
In blood and ash
In home-made bombs
For songs and sons to come –

When all else burns
The night remains.

– Here's to the night.

Scene Thirteen

HELEN. *(laughing)* Here's to the night!

ALL. The night!

*(Lights, music, action. The camp is completely trans-
formed into a 1940s movie set.* **HELEN** *is in a gorgeous
evening gown. A big-band jazz ballad plays. There are
fairy lights and little umbrellas in the drinks. There are
uniformed officers, very handsome, each with a woman.*
LOTTE *stands awkwardly alone on the sidelines, clutching a drink, trying to catch* **HELEN**'s *eye for cues.)*

MENELAUS. I should be angry. I should be furious. But….

HELEN. Shhh. I know. My poor darling. How you've suffered.

MENELAUS. I can't believe…it's really you. It's been forever.

HELEN. I know. All those lonely nights…

MENELAUS. All those lonely nights in the trenches. The
men almost rebelled…

HELEN. Oh, those long, aching nights. But at last…we've
found each other again. I almost gave up hope, kid-
napped by barbarians. I stayed faithful, you know.
The days…interminable. The nights…unbearable.
But deep down, I knew you'd rescue me.
That some day, my Prince would come.

MENELAUS. I really should be angry, Helen.

HELEN. Sorry.

MENELAUS. My naughty little kitten.

HELEN. Kiss me.

MENELAUS. Not in front of the officers.

HELEN. I demand it. Kiss me.

*(He kisses her. They swirl into one another's arms
and, along with the other couples, dance. A completely
Hollywood moment as we swirl into* **HELEN**'s *trium-
phant party dance. Meanwhile, the bartender and his
bar disappear, leaving* **LOTTE** *alone with her drink on
the sidelines.)*

(**TALTHYBIUS** *enters, covered in blood, bearing the broken body of ASTYANAX – i.e. the dismembered doll previously carried by* **ANDROMACHE**.)

TALTHYBIUS. Madam –

HELEN. Darling – Take me away from / all this.

LOTTE. Excuse me, Helen –

(**MENELAUS** *sweeps* **HELEN** *into his arms, like a new bride, and they leave with shameful speed, blowing past* **LOTTE** *like a tornado past a shopping cart. The other dancing couples disappear.*)

(**TALTHYBIUS** *and* **HECUBA** *stare at each other across the immeasurable gulf of the stage.*)

TALTHYBIUS. Madam. Your grandson.

Scene Fourteen

(**LOTTE** *is surreptitiously trying again to get cell phone reception. She is on her stomach, with just a flashlight, like a heroine in a Nancy Drew adventure. She stage-whispers by stage-flashlight.*)

LOTTE. Hello. Hello? Oh, is that the United Nations?... What do you mean, they've been bombed?...The British Embassy...The. Brit-ish. Em-bas-sy.

– Hello?...Oh, thank God. Can you send someone? I'm in some kind of potential rape camp...No, I said "Potential"...About thirty of us...No, the rest are foreigners – I mean, local women. When can you / – (get here)

(**MICA** *snatches* **LOTTE**'s *phone, smashes it on the ground and stamps on it. The camp floodlights go on, revealing* **HECUBA** *with the corpse of* **ANDROMACHE**'s *child, stroking his hair.* **HECUBA** *is wearing* **POLLY X**'s *beer bottle-top necklace.*)

LOTTE. Was that really necessary.

MICA. I told you. No phone calls. No lawyers.

LOTTE. This is outrageous. I have rights, you know. I am a British citizen, and what's more I was on a holiday which I had saved up for, for *two years* –

(**MICA** *raises his hand.*)

MICA. And keep it shut this time, or I'll gag it.

(**MICA** *walks off.*)

HECUBA. You managed to terrify a whole army –
that's quite an achievement for a toddler.
What shall we write on your gravestone?
"The Argives killed this little boy
Before he reached school age
Because they feared his revenge"?

LOTTE. *(to HECUBA, timidly)* I do hope I'm not intruding.
But, as it happens – I have quite extensive experience
with this kind of repair work.

– May I…?

*(LOTTE starts to put the limbs together, gently and
expertly.)*

HECUBA. The last, the last child of Troy –

LOTTE. – He'll be as good as new in no time, won't you
angel?

HECUBA. The future crumples up like a wet paper bag in
our hands.

LOTTE. – Oh, he *has* been torn about. We can't do much
about the skull, but the torso…

HECUBA. Well, my darling, we'll do the best we can.
Not that I think the dead care what we do for them.
But it's terrible for the living, to throw the dead away
as if their lives had meant nothing.

LOTTE. Why don't you try to fit the feet back in, it's a
simple ball-socket – the ankle's a bit tricky, you have
to push…there…and I'll do what I can for the face.
At least his Mama's going to recognize him now, that's
something.

*(LOTTE and HECUBA work together on the doll/ corpse.
For one moment, the worlds come together. CLEA and
ESME join the others, forming a quiet tableau. It is a
moment of ritual – women working together as they have
done for thousands of years.)*

(Then TALTHYBIUS enters).)

TALTHYBIUS. Madam. The sand storm's cleared. We're
loading up.

CLEA. Where are we going?

ESME. We want to stay together.

TALTHYBIUS. No questions. *(to MICA)* Sergeant –

(MICA takes the body of the child and leaves.)

(The crackle and flicker of flames begins.)

HECUBA. Talthybius!

LOTTE. Where is that man going?

HECUBA. Give him back!

TALTHYBIUS. We dug the pits already. And the city's about to explode.

LOTTE. "Pits"? What do you mean, "Pits"? Mass graves?

HECUBA. I need to bury him myself. Talthybius. You promised.

TALTHYBIUS. Madam. There is no time. The city has been torched. And when it hits the oil tanks –

ESME. The last black wings of Troy –

CLEA. Smoke

ESME. Flames

CLEA. Ash

HECUBA, CLEA, ESME. – All blown away.

HECUBA. My city –

HECUBA, CLEA, ESME. – All my dead, burning.

TALTHYBIUS. Take them!

(MICA returns with JORGE and without the child. They round up the women.)

TALTHYBIUS. Come on, move! All the women aboard the trucks.

CLEA. Where are we going?

ESME. Get your hands off her, you prick!

MICA. Shut up and move, bitch.

(JORGE and MICA herd the women off roughly.)

LOTTE. Just where are you taking us? I demand to speak to an Embassy representative. I have the number plates of the trucks. You can't get away /with this –

TALTHYBIUS. Mica!

LOTTE. *(continuing til whenever MICA silences her with the hood and gag)* – It's a clear breach of human rights. There are organizations that track this kind of thing…

(**MICA** *puts a black hood over* **LOTTE**'s *head, gagging her, and ties her wrists with a plastic snap-cord.*)

MICA. All right, march!

TALTHYBIUS. Leave her here.

(beat)

MICA. Pardon, Sir?

TALTHYBIUS. That's an order. She's not on the list.

(**TALTHYBIUS** *and* **MICA** *leave. The crackling sound of fire grows loud, along with the flickering of flames.* **LOTTE** *shakes in terror. But then...Deus Ex Machina...A British* **OFFICER IN BLUE** *enters with a notebook.*)

OFFICER IN BLUE. Miss Jones? Miss Lotte Greta Jones?

(**LOTTE** *makes incomprehensible noises through her black hood.*)

OFFICER IN BLUE. – Oh, sorry.

(He unhoods her.)

OFFICER IN BLUE. Miss Lotte Greta Jones? I'm from the British Embassy.

LOTTE. Oh, thank God. I thought I was going to die here. We have to go right now, the city's in flames and they've doused / everything in petrol –

OFFICER IN BLUE. Not so fast, Madam.

(The **OFFICER** *gets comfortable with a clipboard, a fold-out stool and a long triplicate form.)*

First, I'd like to see your British passport and some secondary form of identification, preferably with a recent photograph. And I need to get you to sign an indemnity waiver and fill out a few simple forms. And then I should like to ask you a few questions.

(Sound of bombs and explosions. Fire. Lights.)

Scene Fifteen

(Two weeks later. Back in Reading, England, at **LOTTE**'s *doll hospital. There are cases of dolls in various stages of repair. There is a large bin full of plastic doll parts.* **LOTTE** *enters, a little bruised and Band-aided, but clean and in new clothes. She picks up a porcelain doll [identical to* **ANDROMACHE**'s *child/doll, but unbroken] and, in the manner of a TV cooking show host preparing a recipe, works with it a little before addressing us.)*

LOTTE. There…that's it…you'll be as good as new soon, won't you my beauty. You're going to make your Mama very happy. She'll be amazed at how well you've scrubbed up…

(to us) You know, I never wanted all this fuss. I'm quite a private person. But really, the only way to meet interesting people is to get involved in life. And I certainly did that! I just wasn't prepared for all the media attention. "Brave citizen facing terror" and all that rubbish. I never felt like that at all, more like I just landed in a mess and muddled through. Not that different to the rest of life really. I'm just glad to be home, back to piles of bills and the terrible English weather! – No, really, I'm happy to get back to work.

(returning to doll) These older models are so fragile. You can do anything with the modern plastics, they just bounce right back, but these porcelain dolls –
It's their rigidity, there's no "give" in the materials. One false move and they shatter.

(Beat. **LOTTE** *slowly puts the doll down.)*

The only part that really disturbs me is, with all the media hoo-hah, they never asked about the women. About where they were taking them in the trucks. And I don't know how to find out. Nobody asked anything about the women. It was all focused on me, goodness knows why, I mean I didn't really do anything except manage to get rescued! Thank God. I guess in time

LOTTE. *(cont.)* everything will feel normal again, and the memories will fade, but it's like they just drove off into a big black hole or something, and that does distress me – *(suddenly seeing the* **BAG LADY***)* – Oh.

(A **BAG LADY** *enters on a gust of rain and howling wind. It is* **HECUBA**. **LOTTE** *does not recognize her.* **HECUBA** *is wearing contemporary rags and* **POLLY X** *'s beer bottle-top necklace. She is soaking wet and looks deranged, as if she had crawled into the 21st century from the bottom of the ocean.)*

LOTTE. Um – Madam. Madam? Can I help you?

HECUBA. Where are they?

LOTTE. Um – pardon? Where are who?

*(**HECUBA** goes to the large plastic bin of doll parts and starts digging.)*

LOTTE. Madam, please, don't touch the dolls – Are you looking/ for something?

HECUBA. I can hear him crying. Ah – he's hiding in all this plastic junk!

(She flings doll parts to the floor as she searches.)

LOTTE. It's not junk!!! Stop that. Stop it at once!

HECUBA. Gone, all gone – I know he's here somewhere. I can smell it.

LOTTE. Please. You must stop that.

HECUBA. I followed the trail!

I survived the desert, then the sea.

I clawed my way up the mast

and howled like a dog for my babies.

*(**HECUBA** sees the porcelain doll and moves towards it.)*

LOTTE. No! You mustn't touch!/ It's fragile –

HECUBA. My eyes spouted fire. My heart, consumed by flames burned to a black lump of coal. Nothing can stop me now. I refuse to die before I've buried them. GIVE ME MY CHILDREN'S BODIES!

LOTTE. Get away from me! This is a precious antique, it's not even insured – Help!

*(A hospital worker rushes in. It is **TALTHYBIUS**.)*

TALTHYBIUS. Madam.

HECUBA. *(to **TALTHYBIUS**)* You promised me. You promised.

TALTHYBIUS. *(restraining **HECUBA**)* I'm so sorry about the disturbance. – Come along now, Ma'am, we'll get you back home and cleaned up.

*(**POLLY X** becomes visible in her space in the gods. And she is not looking at the scene before her, but considering her sculpture – the giant pink heart bordered with broken doll parts, which is now almost finished. **HECUBA** sees **POLLY X** and stares at her, completely transfixed. The others don't see **POLLY**.)*

POLLY X. Something's still missing. *(directly to **HECUBA**)* What is it?

TALTHYBIUS. *(to **LOTTE**)* She gets like this.

*(leading **HECUBA** off)* Come on, Ma'am, back to the Centre. We'll get you a bath and a nice cup of tea – *(to **LOTTE**)* I do apologize for the intrusion.

LOTTE. Don't mention it. No real damage done.

*(As they exit, we hear the loud sound of pouring rain. **LOTTE** turns to see the two figures back-lit against a violent blue sky. **TALTHYBIUS** unfurls a blue umbrella over **HECUBA** and himself as they leave.)*

*(Together, from under the blue umbrella, **TALTHYBIUS** and **HECUBA** turn and look at **LOTTE** from the far past or the near future – then they step into the rain and are gone, like the last fragment of a dream. **LOTTE**, very shaken, snaps herself out of it.)*

LOTTE. God, you don't even have to leave home to have adventures, do you.

*(She gets on her knees and begins patiently picking up the doll parts that **HECUBA** has scattered.)*

POLLY X. What *is* it? What's missing? *(beat)* Oh! DUH!

*(**POLLY X**, facing outward to us, steps against the giant heart so it frames her. **JORGE** and **MAX** appear as shadowy sacrificial attendants on either side.)*

*(A dimly lit CHORUS of **CLEA**, **ESME**, **ANDROMACHE**, **HECUBA** and **CASSANDRA** appear, in a separate space of the gods. They watch **POLLY X**.)*

POLLY X. I don't care about History. It's full of dead people. I just wanted to live.

*(**POLLY X** lifts her arm in defiant salute; **MAX** and **JORGE** stretch a red ribbon across her neck. This is very stylized and not "realistic." Then they pull it tight, sharply. **POLLY X**'s head falls to the side, her throat cut. It bleeds. She is dead.)*

*(The men disappear. White fairy lights, like **HELEN**'s garden party dream, or at a tacky Vegas show, light up round the perimeter of the heart.)*

*(The image of the dead girl framed by the pink heart, surrounded by broken doll parts, glows garishly, while a world away, **LOTTE** continues patiently picking up broken doll parts from the floor of her doll hospital.)*

(Then the little festive lights go out, one by one.)

End of Play

OTHER TITLES AVAILABLE FROM SAMUEL FRENCH

GOD'S EAR

Jenny Schwartz

3m, 4f / Drama

God's Ear marks the debut of Jenny Schwartz, "an indelibly clever play-wright, possessed of linguistic playfulness and a lively sense of rhythm" (*The Village Voice*). Through the skillfully disarming use of clichéd language and homilies, the play explores with subtle grace and depth the way the death of a child tears one family apart, while showcasing the talents of a promising young playwright who "in [a] very modern way [is] making a rather old-fashioned case for the power of the written word" (*The New York Times*).

A husband and wife have trouble coping with the loss of their son, they find themselves speaking in cliches and the husband travels to forget. The wife stays with their daughter and the tooth fairy and tries to figure out how to cope from home.

Winner of the 2007 Susan Smith Blackburn Prize.

"A triumph! An adventurous, arresting new play!"
– *The New York Times*

"An original and inventive theatrical experience…brilliantly written and staged!"
– *The Associated Press*

"Magnificent!"
– *Time Out New York*

"What a remarkable new voice!"
– *Newsday*

"*God's Ear* packs a wallop! An intriguing, haunting and moving play."
– *Back Stage*

OTHER TITLES AVAILABLE FROM SAMUEL FRENCH

WE ARE NOT THESE HANDS

Sheila Callaghan

Drama / 1m, 2f / Simple Set

Ever since their school blew up, Moth and Belly have taken to stalking an illegal internet café in the hopes of one day being allowed in. They take particular interest in Leather, a skittish older man doing research in the café.

Leather is a self-proclaimed "freelance scholar" from a foreign land with a sketchy past and a sticky secret. Leather begins to fall head over heals in love with Moth... but what about Belly? This play explores the effects of rampant capitalism on a country that is ill-prepared for it.

"Bold and engaging, *We Are Not These Hands* is as fun as it is engaging...Rich in detail and full of humor and pathos."
– *Oakland Tribune*

"Swaggering eccentricity...Callaghan takes a lavish mud bath in a broken language...Ripe apocalyptic slang; at its best, it's racy and unrefined, the kind of stuff you might imagine kids in the back alleys of a decaying world might sling around."
– *The Washington Post*

"The gap between rich and poor yawns so wide it aches in Sheila Callaghan's *We Are Not These Hands*, but much of the ache is from laughter. *Hands* is a comically engaging, subversively penetrating look at the human cost of unbridled capitalism on both sides of the river... the anger of the play's social vision is partly concealed by its copious humor, emerging more forcefully after it's over...*Hands* bristles with bright, comic originality, particularly in depicting the limitations of its people."
– *San Francisco Chronicle*

OTHER TITLES AVAILABLE FROM SAMUEL FRENCH

DEAD MAN'S CELL PHONE

Sarah Ruhl

Dramatic Comedy / 2m, 4f / Unit Set

An incessantly ringing cell phone in a quiet café. A stranger at the next table who has had enough. And a dead man—with a lot of loose ends. So begins *Dead Man's Cell Phone*, a wildly imaginative new comedy by MacArthur "Genius" Grant recipient and Pulitzer Prize finalist, Sarah Ruhl, author of *The Clean House* and *Eurydice*. A work about how we memorialize the dead—and how that remembering changes us—it is the odyssey of a woman forced to confront her own assumptions about morality, redemption, and the need to connect in a technologically obsessed world.

"Satire is her oxygen...In her new oddball comedy, *Dead Man's Cell Phone*, Sarah Ruhl is forever vital in her lyrical and biting takes on how we behave."
– *The Washington Post*

"Ruhl's zany probe of the razor-thin line between life and death delivers a fresh and humorous look at the times we live in."
– *Variety*

"[Ruhl] tackles big ideas with a voice that entertains"
– *NPR*

"...Beguiling new comedy...Ms. Ruhl's work blends the mundane and the metaphysical, the blunt and the obscure, the patently bizarre and the bizarrely moving."
– *New York Times*

CPSIA information can be obtained at www.ICGtesting.com
Printed in the USA
LVOW10s0523300414

383812LV00018B/197/P